A LOOK AT LIFE CYCLES

Mammal
Life Cycles

BY BRAY JACOBSON

Gareth Stevens
PUBLISHING

CRASHCOURSE

Mammal Makeup

Many animals you know are mammals! Dogs, horses, elephants, and thousands more are mammals—including people! Mammals are **warm-blooded** animals with backbones. They have hair or fur. Mother mammals make milk to feed their babies, and most give birth to live young.

Make the Grade

Young mammals often stay with their mother a long time, learning how to find food or move with their animal group.

monkey

dog

elephant

pig

horse

5

Mammals can live in many **habitats**, from the ocean to the rainforest. They can be huge, like the blue whale, or tiny, like the bumblebee bat. No matter where they live or their size, most mammals follow a similar life cycle.

Make the Grade

A life cycle is the basic steps an animal goes through as it grows and changes during its life.

bumblebee
bat

blue whale

7

Making More Mammals

In order to **reproduce**, mammals must find a mate. Male and female mammals have many ways of drawing a mate. A male dolphin may swim with a female, or the pair may pet each other with their fins!

Make the Grade

A mate is one of two animals that come together to make babies. Males **fertilize** the eggs females have inside their body.

Mammal babies grow inside their mother. Most mammals are placental mammals. The mother grows a special **organ** called the placenta, which feeds the baby as it grows. How long the baby grows inside its mother depends on the kind of mammal.

Make the Grade

A dolphin baby grows inside its mother for between 10 and 17 months!

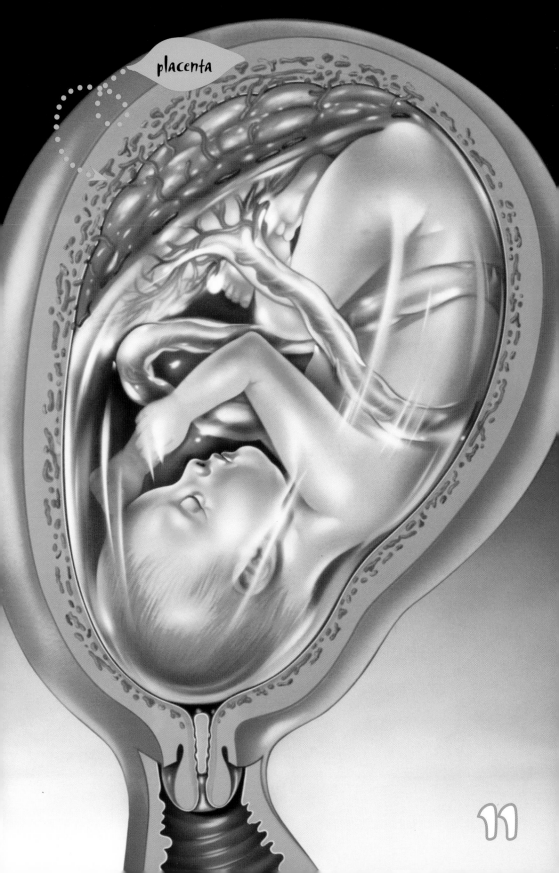

It's Alive!

Most mammals give birth to live young. Some newborn mammals are more **developed** than others. Bear cubs don't have hair and can't see. Horses can stand a few hours after being born! All mammal babies drink milk made in their mother's body.

Make the Grade

People often only have one baby at a time, but other mammals may have more. Big dogs can have up to about 10 puppies in a **litter**!

13

Family Time

Like many mammals, dolphin babies, or calves, stay with their mother even after they've stopped drinking her milk. Mammal mothers, and often others in their animal group, care for their babies. They try to keep them safe!

Make the Grade

Dolphin calves may stay with their mother as long as 8 years!

All Grown Up

It commonly takes mammals years to grow into adults. Most get bigger, and some have changes in their body as they **mature**. Once mammals are developed enough to reproduce, the life cycle starts again!

Make the Grade

Bears are ready to mate, or come together to make babies, when they're 4 or 5 years old.

The Life Cycle of a Dolphin

Adult dolphins mate.

A calf grows inside its mother.

The mother dolphin gives birth to a live calf.

The calf drinks its mother's milk and grows.

The young dolphin develops enough to reproduce.

Pouch Life

Mammals such as koalas and kangaroos are called marsupials. Their life cycle is a bit different from other mammals. Their babies are born even less developed than other mammal young. So, they spend a long time with their mother before they can **survive** on their own.

Make the Grade

The Virginia opossum is a marsupial that lives in the United States and Canada.

A koala baby, or joey, grows inside its mother's body for about 35 days. It's only about 0.8 inch (2 cm) long when it's born! It has no ears and can't see. Still, the joey climbs into its mother's pouch all by itself!

Make the Grade

All marsupials have something like a pouch, but not all marsupials have a full pouch like the koala and kangaroo do.

joey

21

A joey lives in its mother's pouch for up to 6 to 7 months. It only drinks its mother's milk. Once grown enough, it leaves the pouch. Until it's about a year old, the joey rides on its mother's back!

Make the Grade

Koala mothers only give birth to one joey at a time. A joey may stay with its mother longer than a year if she doesn't have more young right away.

The Koala
Life Cycle

Koalas mate.

A mother koala gives birth to an undeveloped joey.

Young koalas may stay with their mother.

The joey climbs into its mother's pouch to drink milk.

The joey leaves the pouch to ride on its mother's back.

The joey grows and develops.

Egg-Laying Mammals?

One group of mammals has one very different step in its life cycle. Mammals called monotremes lay eggs instead of giving birth to live young. Monotremes include the platypus and four kinds of echidna.

Make the Grade

Monotremes are found only in Australia and New Guinea.

platypus

25

After echidnas mate, an egg grows inside the female for about 23 days. Echidna mothers develop a pouch when their baby is growing inside them. They lay their egg into this pouch. Echidnas only lay one egg at a time.

Make the Grade

When baby echidnas, called puggles, are born, they can't yet see. They also have no hair!

echidna
puggle

After about 10 days, the baby echidna **hatches**. Like a baby marsupial, it's very undeveloped. The newly hatched baby drinks milk in its mother's pouch for 2 to 3 months. Once it starts to grow **spines**, the mother takes it out of the pouch.

Make the Grade

Echidnas are covered in sharp spines and fur. The mother takes it out of her pouch because the spines start to poke her!

29

The Echidna
Life Cycle

The young echidna leaves the pouch and soon goes off on its own!

Adult echidnas mate.

An egg grows in the female.

The baby echidna grows spines and fur.

The mother echidna lays an egg.

An echidna baby drinks milk in its mother's pouch.

The egg hatches.

Glossary

develop: to grow and change

fertilize: to add male cells to a female's eggs to make babies

habitat: the natural place where an animal or plant lives

hatch: to come out of an egg

litter: a group of baby animals born at the same time

mature: to become an adult

organ: a part inside an animal's body

reproduce: to create a baby

spine: one of many stiff, pointed parts growing from an animal

survive: to live through something

warm-blooded: able to keep the body at a steady temperature no matter what the outside temperature is

For More Information

Books

Amstutz, Lisa J. *Mammals*. North Mankato, MN; Capstone Press, 2017.

Rudolph, Jessica. *Platypus*. New York, NY: Bearport Publishing Company, Inc., 2018.

Websites

Saint Louis Zoo: Mammals on Our Web Site

www.stlzoo.org/animals/abouttheanimals/mammals/listallmammals/

Discover many cool kinds of mammals—and plan a trip to visit them at the St. Louis Zoo!

Publisher's note to educators and parents: Our editors have carefully reviewed these websites to ensure that they are suitable for students. Many websites change frequently, however, and we cannot guarantee that a site's future contents will continue to meet our high standards of quality and educational value. Be advised that students should be closely supervised whenever they access the Internet.

Index